Manifesting a

The Beginners Guide to The Law of Attraction, Quantum Physics, and Getting What You Want

Lisa Townsend

Table Of Contents

Introduction

I want to thank you and congratulate you for downloading "Manifesting a Miracle: The Beginners Guide to Law of Attraction, Quantum Physics, and Getting What You Want."

This book contains proven steps and strategies for how to be a Miracle Maker, creating health, wealth and abundance in this hologram we call life. If you are reading this book, it is not by accident. You may think that you have just happened upon it. However, because of the Law of Attraction, you really have attracted it to yourself. You probably don't realize it, but this is what you have done.

The Law of Attraction is already working within you and through you. You have created your own reality. The secret is, consciousness and energy creates all reality. You've been creating your reality up to now; now you can create the reality that you want.

Have you ever wondered why some people seem to have everything that they have ever wanted? We all know people who seem to have the ability to make everything they touch turn into gold. Have you found that you ask yourself questions in the mirror like, "What in the world is wrong with me?"

How many times have you walked down the street and seen the car that you wanted, but have never been able to obtain it? How many times have you seen a gorgeous home, and wished for one just like it?

How many times have you said, "I would like to be a part of the 'haves' instead of the 'have-nots.' I don't have to keep up with the Joneses, I just don't want to live paycheck to paycheck anymore."

Having things can be great, but maybe you just want to live a peaceful day. You don't want to wake and run before dawn. You want to sit and relax with your family, and enjoy a simple breakfast. Maybe you want to sit on the porch in the evening, and watch your children play, without feeling that you are neglecting the things they need by not working overtime or getting a second job. Yes, having more than you could ever dream of can be great, but what if everything you've ever dreamed of is coaching your son's soccer team, or really getting to know your family?

Whatever your dream is, no matter how big or how small, it's possible through Science and the Law of Attraction.

The answer to the age-old question of HOW lies in the pages of this book. We are going to explore the unlimited possibilities that reside within you. You don't have to find or buy anything to get it, because everything that you need is already in you, running in your veins, and embedded in your very DNA. We are going to change the question from, "Why can't I," to the exclamation of "Yes, I Can!"

When Neo, from the movie *The Matrix*, asked the question, "Why do my eyes hurt?" Morpheus replied, "Because you've never used them." So get ready, because up until today you have been running on automatic; moved and controlled by the perception of your environment, and held hostage by the illusion of your reality. Today begins your training as a Divine Miracle Worker and Master of Manifestation.

This book is going to act as a tool, an instrument to be used for manifestation. Many of you are just starting to learn to use your manifesting muscles. This book is going to act as a guide

5

to help you hone and manage your consciousness and energy so they work *for* you rather than against you. The length of time you use it will depend greatly on you, and the length of time that you need to manifest your dreams and desires. Every person will manifest according to his or her faith as co-creators with "I am" (we'll talk more about this in a minute…).

For now, thanks again for downloading this book, I hope you enjoy it!

Lisa Townsend

The Electromagnetic Mustard Seed, the Quantum Particle, and the Law of Attraction

So how far down the rabbit-hole do you want to go?

To start with, we need to understand that our great earth has provided the source of "attraction" by its spinning.

The iron core of the earth, as well as its spinning rotation, cause magnetic energy to spring up out of the earth into your Root chakra, which starts at the soles of your feet. This dynamic, compounded with the wave form energy we call light, gives us the phenomenon of an electromagnetic atmosphere.

The sun, as it shines on us, provides further information through wave form energy into our DNA. However, we cannot forget that the wave form energy we call light is also the wave form energy of our DNA. Your DNA, which is a gelatinous mold, is filled with light code configurations. Those configurations are packed with information, pulling to it those things that your spirit/energy has determined are necessary for its survival.

Your DNA is the mustard seed of attraction. It has within it the core elements of creation. Sacred scriptures confirm scientific discovery in the apostle Paul's writing to the church at Rome. Paul understood their greatness, and vast wealth, so he thought it was important to remind them that the law of attraction works for everyone. In Romans, the 21st chapter and the 3rd verse, you will find these words:

> *Rom 12:3 For I say, through the grace given unto me, to every man that is among you, not to think of himself more highly*

than he ought to think, but to think soberly, according as God hath dealt to every man the measure of faith.

What is the measure of faith?

This measure of faith is encoded into your DNA. Every human has some level or magnitude, and the ability to attract based on the electromagnetic energy of the 3rd dimension and their DNA in a makeup.

Matthew 17:19-20 says, *then the disciples came to Jesus privately and said, "Why could we not drive it out?" And He said to them, "Because of the littleness of your faith; for truly I say to you, if you have faith the size of a mustard seed, you will say to this mountain, 'Move from here to there,' and it will move; and nothing will be impossible to you.*

Mark 11:23 says, *For verily I say unto you, That whosoever shall say unto this mountain, Be thou removed, and be thou cast into the sea; and shall not doubt in his heart, but shall believe that those things which he saith shall come to pass; he shall have whatsoever he saith.*

These verses show that Jesus, as a Metaphysician, was trying to explain to his students the scientific principle of the Law of Attraction. First, it is important to note that this teaching was not for everyone. Notice, the text said that the students came to him privately, and asked, "why is it that we could not do this?"

Christ said unto them because of the littleness of your faith.

Let's stop here, and ask ourselves a question. What is faith? Well, Paul in his attempt to explain the law of attraction to the Hebrews said *"faith is the substance of things hoped for and the evidence of things not seen."* In other words, faith is the manifestation of our emanations, and the realization of our imagination.

So what are the metaphysical principles of the Law of Attraction? First, you must have faith, which is something we almost all have. If your faith is only the size of a mustard seed or quantum particle, you can still move mountains.

Secondly, he taught them that if you "say...." "Say" is the principal of speaking the vibration into the atmosphere of the electromagnetic field to attract those things you seek to manifest. The "saying" is the exercising of the fifth chakra (the Vishuddha in Sanskrit), also known as the throat chakra. It has a vital role in the manifestation process. Speaking is a key element in the process of attracting in an electromagnetic environment because of the nature of vibratory frequencies.

It is important to understand that words are simply sound vibrations emanating from the fifth energy center, the throat chakra. That being said, the metaphysical teaching of vibrations, and the word is represented by John, a student of Jesus in metaphysics when he said...

> *John 1:1 "in the beginning was the word and the word was with God and the word was God and the word became flesh and dwelt among us."*

Another way of saying that is, in the beginning was the vibration, and the vibration was with God, and the vibration was God, and the vibration became flesh through entanglement and coagulation of light code configuration creating DNA.

So now, the light code configurations of vibrations are dwelling with us and are us, the waveform energy of humans. With the potential to attract anything, it desires into its

9

experience and journey here on the third dimension that we call earth.

So, we have secret teachings of Jesus to his students concerning the potential of the mustard seed. Secondly, we have the principle of speech using vibrational frequencies to bring things into existence, which is also the teaching of affirmation. We will discuss affirmation in a later chapter.

There is one other principle that we have not yet covered concerning the electromagnetic mustard seed. It is one that is elusive, but can be spotted by the keen eye. It slips the attention of our religious leaders, pop-culture books, and popular films that try to explain it. It is the scientific principle of work or doing. Sacred texts teach us that faith, whether the size of a mustard seed/quantum particle or a colossal 3rd dimensional mountain, is dead without "works" or ACTION.

This means in order to operate within the matrix of the third dimension, you must *do* something to bring about the realization of your imaginations. So it is you, the co-creator, charged with the responsibility of multiplying and replenishing the earth, that must do the doing. So it is you who must have the faith, and it is you who must do the work.

Let's go back and review the process of the Law of Attraction and your mustard seed/quantum faith.

Here are the things that we find.

1. We all have a measure of faith. Because the Earth is spinning and interacting with other spinning planets, the dynamic of magnetism is created. In addition, light from the sun produces sun rays which have

information in them. That information is encoded into your DNA.

2. Vibration is what causes particles to come together or fall apart.

3. Belief is the architect of the things to come. Remember that the sacred texts tell us that as a man thinks in his heart is what he is.

4. You have to DO something. You have to put in the work, because attraction needs action, and nothing from nothing leaves NO-THING.

Before we move on, take a few moments to write down on a piece of paper, or type on your computer what you really desire most in life. This will be the beginning of your vision board.

Make sure to be clear about your desires. Write what you want to be, but don't phrase it as "I want." Instead, use the statements, "I am."

Examples:

Not : I WANT to be a college graduate.

State: I AM a college graduate.

See how much better it feels to write "I am," than "I want?"

The definition of "want" is "to be without or be deficient in." We don't want to reinforce any lack whatsoever and you'll understand why in a bit. For now, just trust me and write everything as "I am".

Make sure to put down your most important goals. You can refer back to them later.

Once you have your BIG goals down (we'll use them in a later section), make a list of three things you want to see happen over the next seven days.

Examples could be:
- I am attracting a new client this week who will pay me $5000.
- I am drinking a free coffee at Starbucks.
- I am pulling into great parking spots everywhere I go.

Stretch what you think is possible, but remember the key is to make a list of the things that you actually believe ARE possible, and watch them over the next seven days to see what small miracles you can manifest.

What exactly is a Miracle?

A miracle, as defined by the World English Dictionary, means "a wonder or marvel," "a wonderful or surpassing example of some quality," or "an effect or event manifesting or considered as a work of God."

The word "miracle" comes from the Latin word for "wonderful" or "to wonder at", and before that from Sanskrit for "smiling."

We've already covered how you as an individual are a co-creator with God – or the organizing force of the universe.

So a Miracle is merely something wonderful, that is manifested by a god-force (i.e YOU).

The truth is that miracles are *supposed* to happen. They actually DO happen all around us, all of the time.

So why hasn't YOUR miracle happened yet?

When miracles are not happening, it is because there is something wrong with the process. Typically, this is because you as the creator of the miracle are also sending out conflicting energy or vibrations that are interfering with the original intention you sent into the quantum field.

Everyone in the world has the power to emit and read vibrations. The perception the world has is determined by the vibrations that you are sending out at this very minute. Are you confident, hesitant, or uncertain? Everything around you feels and responds to that energy.

So how do we fix this problem, develop a positive relationship with the universe, and allow these miracles to happen?

The "ME" 528 Factor

Hidden from the naked eye, the whole world is vibrating, even down to the green grass you see every day. We don't see the vibrations because the human eye can only see 60 frames per second. The mind can not discern anything moving faster than 60 frames per second, so it views the vibration as "solid".

We end up believing that the vibration doesn't exist, but, just like the green grass, all organic life *is* vibrating. According to *Everyday Health for Life,* the sun is actually beaming the 528 Hz frequency at Earth, and we are resonating with it.

There are nine core frequencies that resonate here in the third dimension (of which 528 is one), and each has its own set of properties.

They look like this:

174 Hz (TI)– The Foundation - this is the lowest frequency and has natural pain relieving properties.

285 Hz (DO)– Quantum Understanding - helps return bodily tissues to their original form and helps restructure damaged organs.

396Hz (UT or UT queant) – Liberation from Fear - has the ability to turn grief into joy.

417Hz (RE-Resonare fibris) – Transmutation - has the ability to undo situations and facilitate change.

528Hz (MI-Mira gestorum)– Miracle Manifestation - has the ability to promote transformation and miracles. This is the exact frequency genetic biochemists use to repair damaged or broken DNA strands!

639Hz (FA-Famuli tuorum) – Relationship Harmonization - has the ability to help reconnect and balance relationships.

741Hz (SO-Solve pollute) – Consciousness Expansion - attributed to solving problems, expressions, and providing solutions.

852Hz (LA-Labil reatum) Awakening Intuition –has the ability to awaken and return spiritual order.

963Hz (SI) – Numinous Accord - awakens your body's senses to their perfect, original state.

Dr. Joseph Puleo discovered a pattern of six repeating numeric frequencies, which he believed was hidden in the the Bible's Book of Numbers, in 1974. The codes reveal a series of six electromagnetic sound frequencies that he believed had corresponded to the six missing tones of the Solfeggio Harmonic scale.

UT, Re, Mi, Fa, So, La, and Si – 6 of the 9 resonant frequencies of the 3rd dimension (Earth)

The 528Hz MI note (or as we call it - the "Me" note) is the Mira-gistorum; the miracle note.

Each note has a vibratory frequency all of its own, and each frequency gives out different energy to bring about different manifestation or results.

This information can help us identify some of the reactions we have to different music.

How you feel hearing a certain piece of music has a direct correlation to the vibrational frequency it is putting out.

This means that new age music has a frequency, rock 'n roll has a frequency, hip-hop has a frequency, jazz has a frequency, and so on and so on.

As we said, the "ME" 528 frequency is that of miracles (Mozart and Bethoven wrote many pieces using 528Hz). It is the frequency of good vibrations which bring about healing, calming manifestation here in the third dimension.

So if you give it some thought, it is not hard to understand the meaning or the effect behind sacred chants. Think about the vibrational frequency of a war cry as opposed to the frequency of a love song. You have to ask yourself, what about the frequency of miracle manifestation? How do we use a frequency? How can we have a practical application of a frequency in our everyday lives?

In the quantum field, like attracts like; or, to use an old idiom, birds of a feather flock together.

This brings us back to the apostle John when he said, in the beginning was the word, or as we discussed that in the beginning was the vibration. And that vibration was God, with God, and became flesh. And you are that vibration.

All of the vibration of nine dimensions of a vertical axis, and the six dimensional musical scale lie within you. You have the power of a co-creator with the miracle vibration embedded in your very DNA.

You don't have to get it, you already *have* it, it is part of your genetic makeup.

In short, your DNA is vibrating with information from the light of the sun, and it has the power to manifest miracles.

I must admit that at times I find it amazing just how many of the world's sacred teachings confirm claims made by science, and how much science confirms sacred teachings around the globe.

In the Judeo-Christian creation myth, we find that all of creation was based on sound.

"By the word of the LORD the heavens were made, their starry host by the breath of his mouth.... For he spoke, and it came to be; he commanded, and it stood firm."

In the Ancient Vedic Upanishads, the syllable "om" is first described as an all-encompassing mystical entity. Hindus believe that as creation began, the divine, all-encompassing consciousness took the form of the first and original vibration, manifesting as the sound "OM," which drove out the darkness and created light. The vibration of "OM" symbolises the manifestation of God in form, and is the reflection of the absolute reality, without beginning or end, and embracing all that exists.

Extrapolating that out, and including what we know about DNA frequency vibration, it is safe to say that the sound frequency matrix is responsible for all manifestation.

Now that we have this information, we need to wrap our minds around this:

Located within a musical scale is the mathematical equation of the Fibonacci sequence leading up to phi (the mathematical equation for manifestation here on the third dimension). This can be clearly seen by looking at a keyboard of a piano.

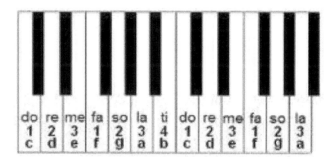

What is the science behind this?

Man is "densified" vibrating matter, which has picked up all of the vibratory frequencies of the mathematical musical matrix scale. Sounds a lot like God manifesting as the vibration Om, doesn't it?

You are a hue-man, coming from a light system or a solar system or a soul system or a sun system. This is why you have a hue, a shade of light – and light comes from sound. Remember... let there be light, and the Om sound driving away the darkness with light.

Light code configurations coming from sound create DNA molecules.

DNA Deoxyribonucleic acid produces RNA- Ribonucleic acid.

RNA Ribonucleic acid produces amino acids.

Amino acids produce proteins.

Proteins produce growth.

So you already have within you the frequency of creation, you are already a qualified co-creator, you ARE the vibratory matrix.

The creative process has been within you from the very beginning of your existence, you just have not used it consciously. No one ever told you that *you* are capable of producing miracles.

However, in your creative process as a co-creator with the universe in the quantum field, your process of manifestation brings light codes *before* sound vibrations (not the other way around.)

Why, you might ask?

You must think of your creation first from the 6th chakra (or the pineal gland, the third eye, or however you identify the 6th energy center). It is there in the pathway of light that you speak what you wish to see manifested. What you see first in your minds eye, you speak through the 5th energy center (the throat chakra) or the vibrational frequency emitter, and that brings about manifestation that you can then see with your physical eyes.

Sacred texts teach that "as a man thinks in his heart, so is he and what he says manifests." They also teach us that the tongue is more powerful than a two-edged sword.

Why is that? The tongue has the power to create and to destroy, because it can harness creative and destructive frequencies faster than the speed of thought.

19

Tapping into the 528 frequency brings us back to the electromagnetic mustard seed. As we explained earlier, just as all men have in them a measure of faith, all men have within them the 528 frequency of miracle manifestation.

How does that work? Remember the Beach Boys song "Good Vibrations"? That is the key. That is what you are looking for, a good vibration.

The secret to the Law of Attraction is not just understanding that you have the frequency within you. It is not just understanding that all men have the measure of faith. It is also the understanding of how you *feel*.

In order to bring about the manifestation, you must feel good about it, that's what the 528 "Mi" frequency is all about. It is the good vibration, or the good-feeling vibration.
When you have the faith to believe something, if you truly believe it, you feel good about it. That good feeling is the confirmation of things hoped for.

You must feel good about what you are trying to manifest. You must have faith to believe in the manifestation. You must then take an action in order to manifest your belief.

Remember, there could be no attraction without action. However, your action must be filled with the good feelings of the 528 vibratory frequencies. The sacred texts back up and support the scientific anomaly by clearly stating "Blessed is the cheerful giver."

This means that you have to have the good vibrations of the 528 Mi frequency in all of your spiritual connections. Allowing yourself to be open, and to give out good vibrations to those you help, truly keeping selfless deeds as they are, selfless, without complaint and with an open heart. Giving and completing selfless acts must come from within, through openness, honesty, and by really meaning the gift as a gift to the universe or to whomever it is your are giving. Complaining about it later, or feeling regret, can disrupt the frequency, therefore allowing greed, regret, or another negative emotion to disrupt the positive influence you are intending into the universe.

This is the concept of Karma; creating a destiny or fate (read result), following as an effect from a cause (your input).

If we are honest, we could say the same thing concerning the ratio of answering prayers. My guess is that only about 15% of prayers are answered, because it's only about 15% of the time that we use the correct formula. Most times doubt is attached to the prayer, causing a lower emitted frequency, that is contrary to the intended purpose of bringing about a miracle of manifestation.

A prayer is not about asking or begging some "higher power" to grant a boon or favor, it is about using your creative powers as they were designed, and co-creating with the organizing force of the Universe.

Eight things YOU must know to create miracles

1. YOU must know that the Mustard Seed/quantum particle is within you.
2. YOU are a co-creator with the Universe.
3. YOU must have faith.
4. YOU must know that faith without action is dead.
5. YOU must do the work.
6. YOU have the Mi 528Hz good vibration frequency of manifestation within you.

Lisa Townsend

7. YOU are embedded with a mathematical musical matrix.
8. YOU and the god force are YOU-NIFIED

The Law of Attraction and The Law of "I AM"

To explore the esoteric meaning of the law of attraction and the Law of "I AM," I want to go to a story from the Book of Exodus in the Torah.

> *Exodus 3:14 …and God said unto Moses, I AM THAT I AM: and he said, Thus shalt thou say unto the children of Israel, I AM hath sent me unto you.*

In the Book of Exodus, we find the story of Moses being commissioned by God to go into Egypt and hold negotiations with the Egyptian Pharaoh. We have heard how he leads the children of Israel out of Egypt, and the miraculous events that took place as they crossed the Red Sea. We have talked about the boils, the locusts, the killing of the firstborn sons, the drowning of the Egyptian soldiers, Moses raising his staff and throwing it down, and it's turning into a serpent, and the Egyptian Pharaoh's servant doing the same thing. We have talked about him lifting his staff and the Red Sea parting.

What we haven't talked about is Moses' apparent insecurities before accepting his mission. Moses could not understand why his god would give him this commission, one that required him to talk to a head of state. Moses didn't understand why God would send him to be bumbling and stumbling over his words on such an important occasion as the freeing of the children of Israel.

Moses told God, "I have a speech impediment, I can't talk straight, I get my words tongue-tied, I can't get them out as I would like. And you don't even have a proper name. Who should I even say sent me?" (At this point in the Scriptures,

God had not been "named" per se. He was known as YHWH, the God of Abraham, the God of Isaac, God of Jacob, and the God of Israel, but not by a proper name.)

Then the God of Moses replied, saying, "I am that I am sent you".

In spite of everything, when it came to God identifying himself, he defined himself as "I am," so therefore "I am" is God.

This is so important that I need to repeat it, "I AM" is the creative god-force of the Universe!

So in Moses' case, it was not about his shortcomings or his inability to construct a cohesive sentence. At the moment when Moses opened his mouth, he was speaking the vibration of "I am." All of those other perceived shortcomings did not matter. Moses was unaware of the fact that he was locked into the mathematical, musical matrix of the 528 vibration "I am."

Let's look at the Christian New Testament for a moment. In the book of John we will find this narrative:

Jesus answered, I have not a devil; but I honour my Father, and ye do dishonour me.[50] And I seek not mine own glory: there is one that seeketh and judgeth.[51] Verily, verily, I say unto you, If a man keep my saying, he shall never see death.[52] Then said the Jews unto him, Now we know that thou hast a devil. Abraham is dead, and the prophets; and thou sayest, If a man keep my saying, he shall never taste of death.[53] Art thou greater than our father Abraham, which is dead? and the prophets are dead: whom makest thou thyself?[54] Jesus answered, If I honour myself, my honour is nothing: it is my Father that honoureth me; of whom ye say, that he is your God:[55] Yet ye have not

24

*known him; but I know him: and if I should say, I know him
not, I shall be a liar like unto you: but I know him, and keep
his saying.*[56] *Your father Abraham rejoiced to see my day: and
he saw it, and was glad.*[57] *Then said the Jews unto him, Thou
art not yet fifty years old, and hast thou seen Abraham?*[58] *Jesus
said unto them, Verily, verily, I say unto you, Before Abraham
was, I am.*

This is a very interesting Bible passage. We find Chrst, the
metaphysician, trying to explain to church leaders of that time
the metaphysical principles of oneness. He was trying to
explain to them that when you see me, you see the father, and
that the kingdom of heaven is within.

The Rabbi, the Priest, the Overseers, the religious leaders,
and all of those who were involved in the religious structure
at that time, did not understand this type of teaching. In their
minds Jesus was a devil. They could not figure out how this
little Jewish Rabbi, with all of these people following behind
him, had gained so much popularity coming against the
religious order of that time. Breaking the religious Laws,
turning over the money-changing tables in the Temple,
working on the Sabbath, hanging out with sinners. Now, to
top it all off, you want us to believe that you and the
Universal Father are of the same oneness. What blasphemy!
So they thought.

In the 51st verse he told them that if you do what I teach,
you will never taste death. He was trying to explain the
metaphysical principle of the hue-man being of the
mathematical, musical matrix as opposed to just a simple
physical structure. They couldn't get it, they said to him, now
we know you are a devil, because our father Abraham is dead.

Christ, the metaphysician, went on to tell the church leaders, you don't know Aba-the father of many nations- Brahma, the breath giver.

You know the myths of our forefather Abram, who later became Abraham.

I know the knowledge of the Brahma. He went on to say, "If I said I didn't see him, then I will be a liar, like you and the rest of the clergy. When I saw him in my day, he was glad and rejoiced to see."

The church leaders still didn't get it, they said to the metaphysician, "How could you have known or seen Abraham when you're not even 50 years old?"

Christ, the metaphysician, replied, "Truly, truly I say unto you, that before Abraham, was 'I am'."

We must remember that, "I am" is God. I am going to try to stay away from the theological inconsistencies and misinterpretations in the texts, and deal strictly with the metaphysical concepts that lie deep within the body of the narrative.

Number one, you must understand and acknowledge that titles in scriptures are mostly principles; God is a principal, Christ is a principal and Lord is a principal.

I've heard many theologians, scholars, and gurus all talk about the principles and the meanings of "I am," and with much content, I have been greatly disappointed with some of the explanations. The language is not universal, especially the English language. Therefore, often times the meaning of "I am" is lost in language.

So we have to go back to the mathematical, musical matrix of vibratory frequencies. To fully understand, "I am," you must have a basic understanding of numerology and its relationship to letters or what we call the Alphabets.

What of the "I"?

A B C D **E** F G H **(I) The I is the Number 9**

The letter "I" is in the ninth position. Nine is the number of completion.

Located in the first nine letters of the alphabet are the first three vowels, or Vows to EL (EL is the Hebrew word for God) = A...E... and I.

To keep you locked out of the secret. The Vows to El (vowels) they left out, where the O, U and Y which = YOU.

The letters A, E, and I contain the same frequencies as three tones from the nine tone matrix (the first middle and last). When used together they are the activation frequency for DNA!

A - 171 – The Foundation – the first and lowest frequency

E – 528 – Miracle Manifestation - has the ability to promote transformation and miracles.

I – 963- Numinous Accord - awakens the senses to their perfect, original state

Using this information "I" = The complete and fully awakened activation frequency of creation.

What of The "AM"?

"AM" is the first person singular for of the *verb* "to be."

A *verb* is a *word* that shows action or being.
"to be" means Existence.

Therefore the action or being of "to be" or "AM" is existence.

I am = I exist

AM is also an Abbreviation of the Latin phrase *Ante Meridian*. Directly translated, it means "before the day" or before the light. Remember, the vibration of the sound Om brought the light of day, so for our purposes AM means before the *manifestation* of god that became god, that included everything and no thing. AM is the field of all possibility – the quantum field.

I am = I exist as the quantum field.

So bringing down our larger definition of "I" from the previous section, and combining it with our new deeper understanding of "AM," brings us the metaphysical definition of "I am."

I am = The complete and fully awakened activation frequency of creation exists as the quantum field.

When you say "I am," it's a clear signal to the universe that you are in creation mode, that you are fully awake and aware, that you are in the quantum field activating vibrational frequencies for manifestation.

The Law states that whatever you add to "I AM" is added unto you.

Whatever you add to "I am" is added to you.

If you say "I am rich", then riches are added to you.

If you say "I am healthy," then health is added to you.

If you say "I am happy" then happiness is added to you.

Likewise, if you say "I am sick," then sickness this is added to you.

If you say "I am poor," then poverty is added to you.

So, when you use "I am" in the negative, that negativity is also added to you, AND YOU HAVE TAKEN THE NAME OF THE LORD GOD "I Am" IN VAIN. The Name Of God is the nature of The Law. Every time You Add Something Negative to "I Am" You Take the name of the Creator In Vain. You are not using the creative power of "I am" to attract into your experience the things that you desire, you are creating against yourself.

Most preachers, teachers, and religious leaders have no clue what this scripture means in the 10 Commandments. The best that they can come up with is not to say the name of God at all, or not use it as a swear word. That is why in some religious traditions, it is blasphemous to say the name of God. It is blasphemous to even spell the name of God in Hebrew, so the vowels (vows to El) have been left out.

Why? Because they have misunderstood the true meaning. It is a clear metaphysical principle of the Law of Attraction, and they have reduced it to remedial dogma!

29

The scriptures teach us to let the weak say, "I Am" strong. If you say "I Am" weak the Law of the Name will give you weakness. So, you say "I am strong," and the law of the name will give you strength.

When the Bible says in the 10 Commandments that God will Not Hold Him Guiltless. This simply means, you don't get a pass because you misunderstood or didn't know. The law is the law, and what goes out comes back. This is also the basis for the Hindu concept of Karma, and for the Wiccan Three-Fold Rule.

Every MIND takes the Name "I Am." We all take the name of the creative force in the universe. Whenever we meet someone or have the opportunity to identify ourselves, the first thing that we say is... 'I Am". "I Am" JOHN, "I AM" JAMES, "I Am" SUSAN, "I AM" ELIZABETH.

We all take the name of the "lord". FROM THIS DAY ON VOW TO NEVER TAKE THE NAME OF THE LORD "I AM" IN VAIN.

YOU ARE THE "I AM." YOU are the "I" that is ante-meridian, A.M. YOU exist as the quantum field. You are part of the "I AM." You are a deriviative of what always has been and always will be. You are the god-force of the universe.

Now that you are coming into the knowledge you must use the instruments and tools presented to you in this book.

You must consciously use the electromagnetic mustard seed, for it is the given faith that is embedded in your DNA. Use that and build upon it until you are operating under the mathematical, musical matrix of the 528 ME frequency creating good feelings that will manifest your miracles.

When you use the Law of Attraction and the Law of " I am," whether consciously or not, you bring to yourself whatever you add to the "I am" (I am Sick, I am Healthy, I am Miserable, I am Happy). Whatever you add, you experience. This may be difficult to comprehend at first, because your muscles as a co-creator may have become atrophied, and you haven't realized you've been creating when you actually have. You may want to start working with the Law to build up those muscles a little bit at a time.

Be conscious of the words you use because they have the Power to create and the power to destroy. Be conscious of your thought process and what you spend time doing.

Why, you might ask?

Because consciousness and energy create all reality. In other words, those things that you are aware of, and those things that you put energy toward are what you are going to be manifesting in your experience – good or bad.

Mind Your Business

Every MIND takes the name "I AM" (we mentioned this earlier but didn't explain it).

One of the most confusing subjects to wrap your brain around, is simply understanding the difference and the dynamics between the brain and the mind. Although they work hand-in-hand (operating to serve the same purpose, the personification of the "I" in the "I am") it is important to understand that they are two separate entities.

A person is the embodiment of characteristics which, when gathered together create a personality.

An embodied personality is a person.

That person is the coagulated thought process of its mind. And locked within the molecular structure of the cells is the energy which was created by the mind.

The brain is the molecular structure that filters the mind. It is the instrument that the mind uses to determine reality based on associative memory. The mind is the energy which allows you to create your reality, the brain is a tool that is used to bring about manifestation. I heard someone say, that if you can see it in your mind, you can hold it in your hand.

When I heard them say that, it made me think about shooting pool - if you can see the shot, the shot can be made. As a pool player I understand, that the key to making the shot is about focusing the mind. If I can hold the vision in my brain, keep my mind's energy behind it, and can see the ball rolling in the pocket, I can make the shot.

Mind focus is the art of manifestation. I understand that I have the other ingredients to bring about the end result.

Understand that you have the talent, that you have the tools, that you use the good vibrations at the right 528Hz frequency and that when you focus you will increase your rate of manifesting.

Why you might ask?

Because at the moment of focus you shut out all outside interference. When you focus you keep the thought in your brain in the 6th chakra (or pineal gland), like a frozen flash in your neural net to achieve your objective.

So what does this all mean?

It means that whatever the mind sees and believes it can achieve.

Think about it, have you ever gone to purchase a car and the salesman tells you to, go ahead sit behind the wheel, see how it feels. Then he goes on to ask, "can't you just see yourself driving this car. I can see you going down the road, and you just look so *good* in it."

You must ask yourself, what is a test drive for?

You are not really testing to see if the car WORKS.

You are having the experience of BEING in that car, and that experience is creating a reality. You have now become aware of what it feels like to sit in that car, see your hands on that steering wheel, hear the roar of the engine, and inhale the scent of new leather seats (if they could figure out a way to

get you to taste it and engage all 5 of your senses without it getting too weird I'm sure they would!).
All of these sensations are now embedded in your consciousness or in your conscious mind. And as we know, it is consciousness and energy that create reality.

And if all Minds take the name of God, "I am" then certainly you have the power to bring that reality as a co-creator in your permanent and long-term experience.

"I AM sitting in my new car…"

Somehow, the used car salesman knows this, but the rest of us have been left in the dark.

The law of attraction is mystical, esoteric and scientific, this can be proven by quantum physics. There are many that say the law of attraction is not mystical. There are many who do not understand the divinity of their own DNA. There are those who have yet to grasp that we were created as a microcosm of the macrocosym of the Universe. It is important to understand that there is a direct conncection between science and spirituality, unfortunately these connections are rarely explored or understood.

Earlier we talked about vibratory frequencies and the fact that everything here in the 3rd dimension is vibrating and spinning, that's why on earth we have night and day, that is why we have seasons, that is why we have magnetism. Everything exists in multiple possibilities at the same time. That is what the concept of yin-yang is, all possibility existing in the whole.

Reality only becomes singular and manifest when we focus on it. Thus focusing brings the object of intention into your reality.

Even the book that you're holding in your hand is vibrating and moving in and out of sight. You do not see it because, your physical eye is not attuned to that that frequency and is only capable of seeing 60 frames per second – much like you don't hear a dog whistle because the sound wave frequency is beyond the range of human hearing. That doesn't mean the sound doesn't exist – it merely means we can't detect it without aid.

The same goes for visual vibrational frequency - since you don't see the movement, you are under the impression that what you are looking at is solid, but it is indeed holographic in nature.

Before we dive further in to the pool of quantum "soup", I want to introduce you to Dr. Fred Alan Wolf, a well known quantum physicist who is also known as Dr. Quantum (you may have seen him in such films as **What the Bleep** and **The Secret**). His focus is the relation of quantum physics to consciousness.

Dr. Wolf performed an experiment that relates directly to our focus here and his results were mind-boggling, for lack of a better term.

In his Double Slit Experiment, Dr. Wolf placed particles in a stimulus free chamber and left them overnight. This experiment happened in two phases. First, with a wall containing a single slit, and then again with a wall containing two slits.

Behind the first wall, is a second solid wall set to record the electrons' landing spots after they pass through the slits of the first wall. The cannon fires the electrons at the slit(s), just like a machine gun. Now, if a machine gun would fire bullets through an opening, you would expect there to be a pattern developing on the second wall where the bullets landed. This pattern should be a rough outline of the opening(s), right?

In the first experiment, with the wall containing the single slit, the electrons hit the wall directly behind the slit, leaving an impression of the slit in the solid wall behind it, just as expected. However in the second experiment, using the wall containing two slits, the results were quite astounding.

In the second experiment, the electrons did not form a pattern on the second wall based on the slits in the first wall. Instead, they made wave patterns all over the second wall, as if they were not fired through the slit projector of the first wall at all. It was as if the electron particles changed to wave particles after they passed through the slits of the first wall.

You have to ask yourself how do they do that, how does something that is solid change to something that is not? Even if you had shot water through the slits there should have been some sort of roughly slit-shaped pattern on the back wall.

So to figure out what was going on and how a particle could change Dr. Wolf did the experiment again.

This time he arranged to have photos taken of each particle as it was fired out of the gun. But when he arrived to check the results the next day, the particles had not changed and formed a pattern on the second wall based on the slits in the first wall, just as you would expect the particle should.

What did this experiment show? It showed us that an electron exists as both a particle and an electron simultaneously. How does that work? Does it exist as an electron when it is not being observed and as a particle when it is being observed?

When an electron is not being observed, it exists in a state of pure potential. Your observation creates reality. Now if electrons are the basic building blocks of all matter, then it is you as the co-creator that is creating your reality based on your observation, and the meaning of that observation to you. This is consciousness and energy in its purest scientific form.

So this brings us to the age-old question, if a tree falls in the forest and there's no one there to hear it, does the tree make a sound?

The Answer: if there is no one there (no observer) there is no forest.

Matter is not manifested until it is observed. And who is observing? You are the observer, that voice in your head, your mind. The next time someone says to you, "it's all in your mind" say, I know!

Yes! I Can

In 2007, community organizer, and Illinois State Senator, Barack Hussein Obama decided to run for the Presidency of the United States. He was about to embark upon a task that was seemingly impossible. If he obtained his objective, he would make history as the first African-American President of the United States of America.

With such a big task in front of him, he needed a powerful campaign machine with a slogan (spoken words), that would resonate throughout all of his supporters to help achieve this goal.

Someone with the campaign came up with the chant, "YES, WE CAN."

"Yes, We Can" resonated throughout the country, it began to take on a life of its own.
Regardless of how you feel about President Obama and his politics, the power of the affirmation, stated simply and repeated passionately, is undeniable, and the media sources showed it. "Yes, We Can" became a global phenomenon.

Let's break this this down, The word "CAN" means "to be able to" or the "power or means to," and is a forward-looking form of "being." It's not "being" NOW but very soon in the future.

Remember our Law of "I AM." "AM" is a form of the verb "to be" which means "to exist" or "to occur."

The Obama campaign was tapping into the power of "I AM," only in a slightly weaker form. I AM means now, I CAN means I will be shortly.

38

There is nothing stronger than the power of affirmations. Whatever you affirm, whatever you can see in your mind's eye, can happen if it's done in the correct frequency with the correct amount of belief. You can make anything happen in the quantum field that will then manifest into your reality. The universe will move people and change events and circumstances to manifest that which you intend clearly and with joy.

How do you use affirmations to change your life? One of the keys to manifestation is the ability to use your fifth energy center, which we talked about earlier, the throat chakra will create your reality. It is the mechanism, the channel if you will, of your spiritual and scientific authority to speak things into existence. Just as a gardener uses a trowel to plant a seed in the earth, you use your throat chakra (the trowel) to speak the affirmation (planting the seed) into the quantum field (the soil).

So how do you harness this energy?

It is actually fairly simple.

In order to allow miracles to happen to you, you have to open yourself up to them. Here are the steps to allowing miracles to take their place in your life.

1. Clarity – You must be clear about what you want. You must open yourself up to what you want, and more. If you do not know what you want, the universe cannot give it to you. If you have to, write down what you want.

2. Remove any obsticals – What is standing in your way? What negative energy are you sending out?

For example, if you want to be a published author, what is standing in your way? Do you know how to write? Do you know the rules of grammar and punctuation? Do you have problems putting your thoughts clearly enough on paper for your readers to understand your concepts?

If the answer is yes to any of these questions, these are your obsticles. Remove them!

Learn how to write, learn the rules of grammar and punctuation, and work on outlining your thoughts before you begin writing. This will ensure that your thoughts are expanded into a story that is clear, open, and engaging.

3. Open yourself up and BE – Being allows the universe to add to you what you desire, because you ARE that. The universe reads your vibrations. Believe within yourself that you are what you want to be. Carrying through with the example of a writer: Even if you are scraping for pennies, realize that is not who you are. You are a best selling author, you are just working toward your miracle.

4. Patience – The universe brings, in its own time, what you need and what you manifest. Just like different types of seeds take different amounts of time to grow and mature, so do your intentions. The key is to be patient and be open to the miracle that you have manifested. Waiting can be difficult, but do not allow this period of time to bring you back to the point of sending out negative vibrations. In other words, don't go out to the garden and keeping digging the seed up to see if it's sprouted – you'll kill the plant!

Manifestation starts from within. It starts with your energy, your belief, and your willingness to create the person, the actions, and the things that you want to be, do, or have.

It is important to understand that in order for the affirmations to work effectively, we must strip away all self-imposed limitations.

For the most part people today are brainwashed into thinking in limited terms.

Remember, whatever the mind tells the body to do the brain will accept it and then will begin to perform according to that command given by the mind.

Henry Ford said, "Whether you think you can, or you think you can't--you're right...."
Whatever your belief is, so be that.

Every person has a measure of faith, and it is according to your faith, according to your belief, how you manifest here in this construct, or in this hologram. If you are going to have unlimited success, you have to open yourself up to unlimited possibilities and unlimited potential use.

What we have to do is become flexible and build our co-creator muscles. Disuse has made them become harsh, brittle, and fragile - almost to the point of breaking; all this has taken place because of self-imposed beliefs and limitations.

So despite what you've heard, despite what you may have read, or which understanding you may have. You need to declare to yourself that all channels of thinking are open; that is, to think, feel, act, and have consciousness of one who has

41

many ways and avenues to which goods and manifestation can reach you, in any area of your life.

That means that you're open to be "added to" economically, healthwise, interpersonally, in your business, and in every other area of your life. You are now open to manifesting your miracles in any area that you desire.

From this day forward, your conscious-mind is a sponge soaking up thoughts from your god-mind, constantly leading you to new avenues of success and experiences. Affirm and confirm every day that your mind is constantly expanding into new horizons of understandings and consciousness, to which new good can manifest through you.

Affirm and confirm that by having all channels open, you see, and manifest good in your life to create ideas or new thought processes. Affirm and confirm that every day you realize that the unseen but very real presence of "I am" is setting into motion energy that draws your desires to you.

Understand this, you have all you need to make your dreams and desires come true at this very minute.

All you need is the belief that it is possible and the will to make it happen.

The purpose of this book is to help open your eyes and give you what you need to convince your mind that you *can* have what you desire.

The idea is to come to an understanding that your mind is part of the universal mind of god, and that it will create circumstances, events, and experiences to bring about the manifestation that you desire.

Through the full power of the all creative, universal mind of God, the quantum field, it has the ability to create all miracle manifestations.

All mystics and wise men throughout history have know that there is but one mind in the universe, and that each individual mind is a part of the one mind that is the universal "I AM" mind.

As a metaphysician, I know that one of the secrets of metaphysical science is daily affirmation. Daily affirmation programs the mind.

Those things that we do repeatedly over and over create new habits, and have the power to bring intentions and desires into reality. With daily affirmation, anything we tell ourselves we are, we become, giving us strength to operate in our highest consciousness which makes it easier to manifest.

If you are living in a one-bedroom apartment, barely getting by, that is not WHO you are.

You are who you DESIRE to be, you just have yet to will it into reality.

So let's take some ACTION!

Step 1 - Think of one of the items on the list you created in the first section (preferably one of the 7-day action items so you can see your results quickly).

Step 2 – Write it down again.

Step 3 – Speak it out loud.

Step 4 – Hold the sound and the thought in your Mind and feel it become reality.

Step 5 – With your eyes open and a soft focus (like a light meditative state) say, into your mirror…

- Yes! I can, because "I AM" one with the universe "I AM."

- Yes! I can, because my mind is one with the spirit of the universe "I AM."

- Yes! I can, because there is one life in the universe, and "I AM" one with the oneness "I AM" that "I AM."

- Yes! I can, because I embrace the unlimited wisdom of the universe "I AM."

- Yes! I can, because "I AM" one in mind with the creative process of the universe "I AM."

- Yes! I can, because "I AM" intuitively guided daily to my success and happiness in life by the universe "I AM."

- Yes! I can, because "I AM" renewed daily in mind, body, and spirit because of the universe "I AM."

- Yes! I can, because I believe in, and accept, the supreme power of "I AM" in all things in my life.

- Yes! I can, because I daily affirm the truth of my oneness with the universe "I AM."

- Yes! I can, because the power of the universe "I AM" in the quantum field is greater than any weakness I may be holding in my physical, mental, emotional, or spiritual being.

- Yes! I can, because I make mental energy contact with the universe "I AM" daily in meditation.

- Yes! I can, because my strength comes from the ever-renewing, ever-regenerating power of the universe "I AM."

- Yes! I can, because through the infinite presence and the wholeness of the universe "I AM," I am able to relate to all people and conditions.

- Yes! I can, because of the perfection of the universe, "I AM" is expressing itself in me in my daily life.

Repeat this process in the morning and the evening everyday for a week and watch for signs of your intention manifesting. Write them down in your notebook.

Affirmations

You might be wondering why affirmations got their own chapter after all of that.

Affirmations are one of the most powerful tools in your tool box for manifesting your desires, obtaining your goals, and to allowing the universe to create miracles in your life!

There have been many scientific studies done, and research proves that every person in this world has approximately 45,000 to 51,000 thoughts every day. This means that you have approximately 150 to 300 thoughts every minute!

Why is this information important?

Because every scientific study completed on thought patterns shows that almost 80% of those thoughts are negative!

What we have also been programmed to believe, is that most of these thoughts are sub-concious and therefore beyond our control.

Affirmations are part of our thought process.

Affirmations make the sub-concious thoughts conscious.

Affirmations make you aware of your thoughts. If they are negative, they show you where you are allowing negative vibrations into your life.

Once you begin making conscious positive thoughts, you become more aware of the piles of negative thoughts that are mucking up your life!

Remember when your mother told you, "Be careful what you think, because what you think is what you get?"

She could not have been more right. You create what you think about.

If you are always thinking about being behind on this bill or that bill, you will be behind on those bills.

Why?

Because those bills are taking time from your thought processes that would allow you to come up with ways to make the money to pay those bills, if you would only focus on THAT.

Remember, you are thinking close to 50,000 thoughts per day. Nearly 80% of those thoughts are negative. To make matters worse, 90% of those thoughts will carry over to the next day and blend in with the negative thoughts of tomorrow. Pretty soon, you are not able to hear even a whisper of a positive thought through all of that noise.

Affirmations allow you to take hold of your thought process and begin crushing the negative thoughts that are clouding your mind. To affirm means that you say something positive and truly believe it. They are a way for you to "will" positive thoughts into reality.

You have the power inside you to will positive things. The only things holding you back are the negative thoughts that are spinning in your head. These same negative thoughts are the one's that make us human and prevent us from using the Law of Attraction. They are what hold us down and hold us back from connecting with the energy that allows us to become more than we are at this very minute.

So how do you stop negative thoughts?

You replace them with positive thoughts and positive energy. Positive thoughts and positive energy are the key to manifestation. They allow you to be, on the inside, what you will be on the outside through faith, patience, and determination.

Turning positive thoughts into a manifestation involves faith and will. If you want to be something, you have to believe deep inside yourself that you *are* that something. Tell yourself that you are, know that you are, and believe that it is possible. Open yourself up to that something… and more. Do not limit the outcome of your manifestation by closing the door after you get what you want.

You need to be open to your goals AND MORE.

Do not allow negative thoughts to come back. Once you have affirmed that it will happen and open yourself, rid yourself of any negative thoughts. There are no WHAT If's, there is only "I AM."

The universe is yours to mold, and your place in it is yours to choose.

What negative thoughts have clouded your mind today? Take those negative thoughts and turn them into positive thoughts. Turn them into solutions, and clear all of the negative filters away that make your life blurry. These filters stand between the person you are now, and the true you of tomorrow.

The key to affirmations is to keep them simple. Each affirmation should reinforce one positive thing at a time.

They should be concrete and to the point. By doing this, you can transform the negative into the positive.

Through our beliefs and will, we can overcome poverty, poor health, uncontrolled weight, and the relationships that we have with other people.

So how do affirmations transform what is now, to what you want to be tomorrow? All of the negative thoughts that have held you back, are what created where you are now. These negative thoughts allowed you to will your current life into reality. Your life is what you have manifested.

Replacing negative thoughts with positive thoughts, and affirming the positive, pushes away the negative vibrations that are controlling your life. Repeated affirmation helps to reprogram the thought processes that restrict your power.

Perception is reality. The way you see the world is the way the world is and will be.

If at any time during the day, you feel negative thoughts creeping up on you, or you feel down for any reasons, reaffirm yourself. Tell yourself the positives, and bring yourself back into a positive mindset. Do not allow negative thoughts to control your life.

What you focus your mind on, will be what you attract.

Three simple rules to affirmations:

1. Only affirm positive thoughts. Avoid asking yourself "what if" questions. Use the words you want to become reality.

2. Make affirmations short and simple statements. You want to be able to list your affirmations quickly and easily. Do not ramble on.

3. Do not force yourself to believe, allow yourself to believe.

Manifestation Playbook

It is a good idea to use this book for at least 30 days. After that, refer back to it to chart your progress. This will allow you to see what you have achieved and what still needs work.

Create your vision board and your life the way you want it to be.

To create the vision board, paste photos of what you want your life to be and claim them. Do not add a lot of writing. Simply state your will. This is my house. This is my car. This is my... whatever it is. It is yours and it will be yours.

Every morning before you leave the house go to your vision board and remind yourself, keep it top of mind (in your pineal gland/ 6th chakra), keep in your focus what you have in your mental reality. Do not read quietly to yourself, but read it out loud. You should get into a habit of reading things out loud, because speaking allows you to make an energetic record in the atmosphere.

Remember, if you say to the mountain, "be thou cast into the sea," and believe in your heart and not doubt, then it shall be cast into the sea. Remember that based on quantum physics, particles and light waves do different things based on observation. Remember to use the 528Hz frequency.

If you are watching and waiting impatiently seeing only the lack, the universe cannot change what you are seeing!

Remember to follow these steps:

1. Clarity
2. Remove any obsticals
3. Open yourself up and BE
4. Patience

Rate your believability level of achieving your goal on a scale of 1-10.

If your belief level is low make an adjustment. Perhaps temporarily lower expectations, or find a new task.

You want your belief to be at an 8 or higher. Work within your belief system and really tap into your ability to manifest.

If you're looking to manifest a free cup of coffee, what is your believability rating?

If you want to attract that new client who will pay you $5000, what is your believability rating?

Rating each thing you are working to manifest will increase your level of belief.

Then write it in a notebook, making notes of all the signs of progress and the eventual manifestation.

You must write it down. Writing it down allows you to create a record. Once you create the record, you can then go back to it and begin to build upon it. Once you can see that the system does work, you can PROVE it to yourself, because you can go back and say, "this showed up on this day, and that happened on that day," and so on. This "evidence file" if you will, will begin to build up the muscles that have been dormant for such a long time. It will strengthen your belief, or Faith, as we discussed earlier.

You have to feel good about what you want, you have to believe that it is possible to create your goals, your objectives, and to gain what you desire.

Clear out all negative energy standing between you and what you want.

You can use tools like Chakra Clearing, and Emotional Freedom Technique (EFT) to help clean up your energy. If you don't, those negative frequencies and vibrations will drive away what you are working to manifest!

Start seeing your goals daily, visualize that they have already happened.

First clear your thoughts, affirm or declare them out.

Write down all things for which you are grateful. Gratitude creates momentum and velocity. See, hear, touch, feel, and verbally describe the event for which you are grateful.

Write in your notebook. Write your emotions down, how you feel about it.

Allow yourself to feel how you are going to feel when theses things happen; relief, joy,
Excitement, whatever.

Do not force your beliefs, allow positive thoughts to gently become beliefs.

When your doctor gives you an antibiotic, you don't force it to work, you simply take it, believe it will work, and put your

53

trust in the antibiotic. Once you believe it will work, you remind yourself of it on a regular basis, and wait for the medication to do what it is meant to do.

The same goes for the universe. Believe you are, know you are, take action, and allow the universe to help you become what you are.

Let whatever shows up, show up. Acknowledge yourself as a deliberate creator.

Be easy in the quantum field; gently intend, and act on those intentions.

Stop begging, there is no one there to grant a wish, *you* are the creator of your life.

So "be" it, then let it go, and start seeing the evidence of attraction in action.

Like attracts like. If you see it in your mind, you can hold it in your hand. Ask it, believe it, receive it.

Conclusion

Thank you again for downloading this book!

I hope it was able to help you gain a better understanding of the power that is within you as a co-creator to manifest miracles in your experience. I trust that your eyes have been opened just a little more, so that you can see the infinite potential that lies within your reach.

Take the principles and the tools here and begin applying them in your daily routine.
The next step is to put your visionboard and notebook together, and start manifesting your miracles.

Finally, if you enjoyed this book, please take the time to share your thoughts and post a review on Amazon. I'd really appreciate it!

Thanks and good luck!

Lisa Townsend

Check out these other books by Lisa Townsend!!

http://www.amazon.com/dp/B00IXCUGWE

http://www.amazon.com/dp/B00IX71JQQ

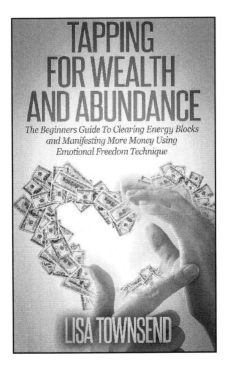

http://www.amazon.com/dp/B00K37EXW6

Printed in Great Britain
by Amazon

43344880R00034